FINDING GOD
In the Storms of Life

FINDING GOD
In the Storms of Life

The Testing of Your Trust

Mike Jones

Copyright © 2009 by Mike Jones.
The scriptures were taken from the New International Version of the Bible.

Library of Congress Control Number: 2009905221
ISBN: Hardcover   978-1-4415-4023-2
         Softcover   978-1-4415-4022-5

All rights reserved. No part of this book may be reproduced or transmitted in any form or by any means, electronic or mechanical, including photocopying, recording, or by any information storage and retrieval system, without permission in writing from the copyright owner.

This book was printed in the United States of America.

To order additional copies of this book, contact:
Xlibris Corporation
1-888-795-4274
www.Xlibris.com
Orders@Xlibris.com
60256

To my wife, Sheila, for holding it together
during this stormy period of loss and uncertainty.
For her repeated encouragement that I should write a book,
then for her patience when I finally decided to do so
as it occupied so much of my leisure time.
And finally, for her input that has helped to eliminate
many of the bumps and potholes
that interrupted the flow of what I wrote.

To my mom, Gail, for her help during the process of editing and review.

CONTENTS

Acknowledgments..9
Introduction..11

PART 1

Distractions to Our Trust

1 Creation's First Void...17
2 Seek Ye First..19
3 The Lure of Good Things...21
4 All that is Ours...24
5 The Dimming of Our Eyes...27
6 We Settle for Crumbs...29
7 Be Anxious for Nothing..31
8 God's Consuming Fire..33

PART 2

Strength for Our Trust

9   Between Two Doors 39
10 Faith Comes by Hearing..42
11 The Battle for Our Faith..45
12 When God Speaks..48
13 The Master's Rage...51
14 Today's Praying...53
15 When Each Do Their Part..56
16 When Jesus Doesn't Come..59
17 Why Do You Wait..62
18 Can You Trust..66
19 A Poetic Prayer..69
20 The Cloud of Witnesses...72

PART 3

Benefits of Our Trust

21	God's Greatest Joy	77
22	Pray without Ceasing	79
23	A Different Path	82
24	What to Do	85
25	God's True Blessing	88
26	Daily versus Grand	92
27	The Well	95
28	"Thy Work—To Rest in Me"	99
29	"Enough That God My Father Knows"	101
30	This My Only Need	104
31	For Those Who Hear His Voice	107

ACKNOWLEDGMENTS

There is a poem included in this book called "When Each Do Their Part." The inspiration for it came from Ephesians 4 where it speaks of the gifts God gave His church. Among them are preachers and teachers. Their purpose is to build up His church so that it would not be tossed about "by every wind of teaching and by the cunning and craftiness of men in their deceitful scheming." As Satan has his tools to deceive and tear down, so God has His to strengthen and build. His body, the church, is held together by these supporting ligaments.

There are several of these gifts and supporting ligaments that have been a source of strength to us in our time of testing. Though we do not know them personally, still I would like to acknowledge the help that their gifts have been to us.

Our DVR is full of T. D. Jakes, Joel Osteen, and Joyce Meyer. Often, at the end of our day, we have watched these recordings. I cannot begin to adequately express the help and strength we received from them. It takes many different tools to build a house. I believe the three I have mentioned are tools God uses to build His. I know He has used them to build us.

As these gifted speakers have provided a good supply of inspiring messages, so others have written good books that do the same. Several that I have read recently have been especially helpful. I have read a few of Brennan Manning's books. In *The Signature of Jesus,* he writes, "The Lord withdraws all tangible supports to purify our hearts, to discern if we are in love with the gifts of the Giver, or the Giver of the gifts." John Eldredge writes in *Walking With God*, "There is no greater tragedy for the human heart than this—to believe we have found life apart from God." Finally, the words of Hudson Taylor in *Hudson Taylor's Spiritual Secret,* "You cannot be your own savior, in whole or in part." I have never read of anyone who trusted God with every aspect of his life more than this man. As a result, he saw God's wonders in his life and ministry.

One more supporting ligament I must mention is Mark Hall and his group, Casting Crowns. In his gifted way, he too communicates the heart of God through music. We have listened to his song "I Will Praise You in This Storm" many times on the way to church. His comments regarding the song are, "Sometimes God calms the storm. Sometimes God chooses to ride the storm with us." God had obviously chosen to ride ours with us.

Thanks to those I have mentioned, who keep the extraordinary aspect of our God before us, I have learned to soar with Him. Because they see Him who is invisible, they have persevered. Their examples inspire us, and because of who He is, we are able to do the same.

Though we know none of these personally, still their God-given gifts have been used to touch us. Two, who we do know, Mark Anderson and Ron Watts, our most recent pastors, may not have the fame the others have, but they know and are known by God. Their passion for Him has inspired us on a very regular basis to want to know God as He is able to be known.

As each does his part, God's church is built up and strengthened. We have been fortunate to have had some of His best influence us.

INTRODUCTION

We receive a lot of cards for special occasions. Most of the time we leave them displayed for a few days, then they're thrown away. Occasionally, if one is really good, we might save it. But one card we still have on display after a year. It may likely remain for another.

We received it about six months into what has now become a test of almost two years. The front of the card shows two doors, one at each end of a hallway. The opening line reads, "When God closes one door, He always opens another," but the tagline is why it is still on display—"But it's hell in the hallway." At that point, for us it was, and we knew it all too well.

It is all about trust. Though a hallway experience is very good testing ground for trust, on a regular basis we face all kinds of trouble and endure all kinds of hardship that can test us just as well. There is no shortage of opportunities for our trust to be tested.

God, who created all we now see and enjoy, still has the same creative ability with which to help us. But often we don't even give Him the opportunity. Satan is very active in distracting us from that trust. In an endless number of ways, he convinces us that God can't. So before we ever go to Him to find out He can, Satan convinces us otherwise.

But God is able, and as Satan uses his lies to distract us from that fact, God has His truth for those who will take the time to listen for it. As we become more and more aware of Satan's goal and tactics, we should be able to recognize them sooner and in turn go to God sooner for His help and truth. When we get to that point in our Christian walk, we are in line for some incredible benefits and wonders.

Our trust is on the line. Trust believes God can. But more than that, trust simply believes God. We all want Him to come in and save the day. Israel wanted out of the desert, but instead, they saw His wonders as He provided for them in it. Just as He wanted them to trust that He would provide what they needed, so He wants us to trust. Instead of crying and complaining about our situation, He wants us to trust that He is in utter control of it and will give us what we need when we need it. Trust believes that.

No matter how long the hallway or severe the storm, God has no limit in His ability to compensate with peace. Paul expressed similar thoughts to the Romans when he said, "Nothing can separate us from the love of God." As hard as Satan will try to feed us lies to discourage us and convince us of our doom, God has abundant life available for those who will come to Him. Jesus said, "If anyone is thirsty, let him come to me and drink." He added, "Streams of living water will flow from within him."

PART 1

Distractions to Our Trust

Our ability to trust God has been tested and tried from the beginning. Satan's goal is to keep us from it. The Bible tells us that Jesus came that we might have life and that we might have it more abundantly. It says if we seek Him first, all that we need will be given to us. But the Bible also warns that Satan's goal is to steal, kill, and destroy. It tells us that he roams about like a roaring lion, seeking whom he can devour.

Satan is very good at distracting us from a simple trust in God, which leads to abundant life, from a simple trust that He is able to supply us with all that we need. Ever before us are things, and if we are seeking them more than we are seeking God, we have become distracted. Jesus says that He is the way to abundant life. Satan suggests that *things* are. It has become so ingrained that we don't even stop to think about it anymore.

It is important to keep the primary goal in mind, which is to seek God first. Satan may use unacceptable things to lure us away from that pursuit, but if we have learned to resist those temptations, he can also use acceptable things to do so. If we have learned over time to choose good things over bad, we have done well. The Bible tells us to choose good over evil. But it is not the end in itself. We can get so wrapped up in the pursuit of good things, thinking we are pleasing God, that we no longer seek Him. If that is the case, we have become distracted.

One other huge distraction Satan uses is worry. Where trust says God can, worry says God can't. The Bible says that God will keep him in perfect peace, whose mind is stayed on Him. If we keep our mind stayed on Him, we are giving Him the opportunity to show us that He can. But if we keep our mind stayed on worry, we are listening to Satan's claim that He can't.

God and Satan are after our trust. The one to whom we listen wins. If we trust what Satan is saying, we will take matters into our own hands because we believe that God can't. On the other hand, if we trust that God can, we will wait on Him.

We are instructed to seek God first. But for most at best, He is in the mix of all the other things we seek. Still it says what it says. We allow the lure of good things to distract and to dim our eyes. We settle for crumbs compared to His best. We allow worry to rob us of the wonders He is so able to do in our lives. If we are habitually distracted by either or both of these, God may send a consuming fire into our lives to burn all the distractions away. It is not pleasant in the beginning, but "no discipline seems pleasant at the time, but painful. Later on, however, it produces a harvest of righteousness and peace for those who have been trained by it."

1

Genesis 2:8
Now the Lord God had planted a garden in the east, in Eden;
and there He had put the man He had formed.

Genesis 2:15-17
The Lord took the man and put him in the Garden of Eden
to work it and to care for it. And the Lord God commanded the man,
"You are free to eat from any tree in the garden;
but you must not eat from the tree of the knowledge of good and evil,
for when you eat of it you will surely die."

Genesis 3:6
When the woman saw that the fruit of the tree was good for food
and pleasing to the eye, and also desirable for gaining wisdom,
she took some and ate it.

Genesis 3:8
Then the man and his wife heard the sound of the Lord God
as He was walking in the garden in the cool of the day,
and they hid from the Lord God among the trees in the garden.

So much He had given them to enjoy. In addition, they also enjoyed the freedom of walking and talking with God. This combination is the source of the most abundant life imaginable.

Satan is always after an angle to distract us from this abundance. If he can get us to turn our attention to these distractions, our attention is drawn away from God. The event in Genesis 3 is the record of the first such occasion (man's first experience with guilt and God's first heartbreak). It is a prime example of what Satan has been doing ever since and why. He knows how much God enjoys walking and talking with us. He knows of the abundance that is ours to enjoy. If he can keep us distracted, his goal is accomplished.

Pleasure is at the root of so much that he uses to distract us. Whether the neighbor's pretty wife, nice house, or good job—it is all presented as something that will be more pleasurable than what we currently have. It is his version of abundance, not God's. Walking with God with what He has given us to enjoy is the real source of abundant life.

Creation's First Void

You planted a garden
where man was to stay.
You met him for walks
in the cool of the day.

But one day they hid
when You called their name;
something was wrong,
it wasn't the same.

Creation's first void—
man's first brush with guilt—
God's first broken heart
since all He had built.

Pleasure the lure
that spoiled what they knew—
the good in the garden
and their walking with You.

Pleasure is still
the distraction of choice,
and hiding our way
when we hear Your voice.

But abundance still there
for those who will choose
the good He allows,
the walks to not lose.

So learn of His ways
and the abundance that stems
from seeking Him first
and walking with Him.

2

Matthew 6:28
And why do you worry about clothes?
See how the lilies of the field grow.
They do not toil or spin.

Matthew 6:31, 32
So do not worry, saying,
"What shall we eat?"
or "What shall we drink?"
or "What shall we wear?"
For the pagans run after all these things,
and your heavenly Father knows that you need them.

Matthew 6:33
But seek first his kingdom and his righteousness,
and all these things will be given to you as well.

It says what it says. Do we do it? Few can say yes. We like to think we do, but most go after things pretty hard and use an enormous amount of energy doing it. Afterward, we like to say He blessed us with it or that He enabled us to get it. The picture painted in these verses is much different from our interpretation.

There is a constant struggle trying to reconcile Christianity, as recorded in the Bible, to our everyday lives. Some are better at it than others, but we all try. The dust eventually settles around the conclusions we've drawn, which become our version of Christianity. We have worked out our salvation.

That is all well and good, or at least, we think it is until God decides to step in and show us His version. Knowing what we have settled for in light of what He had in mind, He may take much away to clear the way for us to see Him. Once our hard drive has been wiped clean and He gives us a new operating system, He then is able to give back some of the things that were taken away. This time, instead of distracting, when He is truly first, they become a source of joy as they were intended to be.

Seek Ye First

"Seek ye first,"
it says so clear,
but the're so many things
that we hold dear.

The pull is strong
in our younger days,
so we split our chase
and go both ways.

It's one or the other,
you cannot have both,
yet we'll try to the death
in spite of our oath.

We say He is first
but He's really not.
He's in the mix.
It's the best we've got.

With no sign of change
He deals us a loss;
our custom-made trial
to pull out the dross.

His goal has been set
and continues to skim;
this He will do
till He can see Him.

He turns up the heat
to burn all away
that we have let in
day after day.

He takes all away
in spite of the pain.
He knows what is best
and what we will gain.

Nothing compares
as He always knew.
The loss clears the way
to knowing You.

3

Revelation 3:17, 18
You say, "I am rich; I have acquired wealth and do not need a thing."
But you do not realize that you are wretched,
pitiful, poor, blind, and naked.
I counsel you to buy from me gold refined in the fire,
so you can become rich; and white clothes to wear,
so you can cover your shameful nakedness;
and salve to put on your eyes, so you can see.

These are some pretty strong words, but if we are of the frame of mind that we are doing pretty well and do not need anything—from God's perspective—in light of how He knows things could and should be, we are wretched, pitiful, poor, blind, and naked.

We're missing His best and do not realize it. We think we are rich because of all the things we possess, but in fact, they have made us poor. They have cost us His presence. We think the good feeling we get from going to church and maybe paying our tithe or doing good things for others is experiencing God. It is just enough to satisfy that part of us that knows some part of our lives should be dedicated to God.

He longs to be our all. For those who have wealth and God, hats off to you. You know who you are and what is referred to here. God is the passion of your life, and the wealth has not distracted you from Him. The one referred to here has allowed God access to a little corner at best and is missing the richest experience possible.

This is where God is coming from. The challenge is there for anyone. No one's life is anywhere near as rich as it could be if he or she was walking with God. It is how we were made. It is what we were made for. Something is missing no matter how rich we become. Compared to what it should be like, many are poor and do not realize it.

The Lure of Good Things

It's not just the bad that keeps us from God,
good will work too, and it's more common than odd.
Good is so plentiful in these days that we live.
We have toys and church and tithes that we give.

We think ourselves rich; that we don't need a thing.
We've been lured into things, being our aim.
I'll admit you have good, but it's cost you My best.
Do you have an ear to hear the rest?

Do you think these things are the best that I've got?
Try buying My gold, and I'll show you they're not.
These things that you seek will one day be lost.
If you have an ear, then let's count the cost.

Things cost you My presence most every day.
They demand all your time and get in the way.
They prevent all My wonders so you will not see.
Your only wonder is why they can't be.

You'll miss My provision when you have a need.
You're too self-sufficient to wait at My feet.
The doors I would open to fulfill My plan,
won't ever be opened with you in command.

Compared to My gold, you're wretched and poor.
You're blind to My best because of good's lure.
I challenge you though to seek Me and see
what true abundance can really be.

4

Genesis 3:1-5
Now the serpent was more crafty than any of the wild animals
the Lord God had made. He said to the woman,
"Did God really say, 'You must not eat from any tree in the garden'?"
The woman said to the serpent,
"We may eat fruit from the trees in the garden,
but God did say, 'You must not eat fruit from the tree
that is in the middle of the garden,
and you must not touch it, or you will die.'"
"You will not surely die," the serpent said to the woman.
"For God knows that when you eat of it your eyes will be opened,
and you will be like God, knowing good and evil."

Matthew 4:8
Again, the devil took him to a very high mountain
and showed him all the kingdoms of the world and their splendor.

He couldn't take it any longer. God and man were having too good a time. He knew how to bring it to an end. It was all just a matter of time. He highlights the good of all that is not best to lure us away from what is. They had it all—the good that God had allowed—and God. That is the best possible combination for abundant life.

But get us to go after something that He has not allowed, and we are pulled away from Him. Satan is the master at showing you the splendor of all that is not best to see if he can get you to bite. The first Adam did. The second Adam (Jesus) didn't.

I will say it wherever fitting, no matter how many times it is repeated—God's greatest joy is walking and talking with us. He desires we know Him well enough that we know His voice and trust Him to provide and care for our lives. He, the Master Shepherd, goes ahead of us to prepare the way for us. We do not have to worry about what we will need; it will be there.

As we come to know Him this well, we'll see His small wonders of provision as we trust and follow Him. Satan will do anything he can to disrupt us from that. If he is successful, we will not experience it. Our Christianity will be flat compared to what it could be. It is so below what our walk with Him is supposed to be. Once you catch a glimpse of what He had in mind, there is nothing you'll want more.

All That Is Ours

Some think of God
as one against pleasure;
there's a long list of don'ts
He expects us to treasure.

But where does it come,
this image in mind?
Who paints this picture
time after time?

Remember the garden,
with Adam and Eve;
Satan's cunning approach
toward them to deceive?

Things had been perfect
up until then;
the two walked with God
as friend walks with friend.

How does it happen
all the good at our door
that Satan is able
to tempt us with more?

He highlights the good
of all that's not best,
to lure us away
from our place of rest.

God's not against pleasure
though there are a few don'ts.
There's good and there's best
and give in He won't.

He still loves the walking
and talking each day.
No pleasure compares
with hearing Him say,

My peace I'll give
if you trust in Me.
Walk with me daily
and my wonders you'll see.

All that I have
I freely will give.
Just seek Me first
and you'll abundantly live.

I know what you need
and I will provide;
just tell Me your heart
and in Me confide.

You won't have to worry
about the few don'ts;
when you walk with Me,
there's no more you'll want.

5

Revelation 18:4
"Come out of her, my people, so that you will not
share in her sins . . ."

Revelation 21:27
Nothing impure will ever enter it,
nor will anyone who does what is shameful or deceitful,
but only those whose names are written
in the Lamb's book of life.

Revelation 22:1-5
Then the angel showed me the river of the water of life,
as clear as crystal, flowing from the throne of God
and of the Lamb down the middle of the great street of the city.
On each side of the river stood the tree of life,
bearing twelve crops of fruit, yielding its fruit every month.
And the leaves of the trees are for the healing of the nations.
No longer will there be any curse.
The throne of God and of the Lamb will be in the city,
and his servants will serve him.
They will see his face and his name will be on their foreheads.
There will be no more night.

    The splendor of heaven would be a good image, of which we should be more mindful. Everything in heaven is pure. Having the image of that purity in mind might and should alter the way we live. The image is easily dimmed. It is Satan's goal to dim it. In my opinion, he has been successful.
    In Revelation, God says to His people, "Come out," which implies that His people can be affected by the ways of the world. It is easy to think we're okay. It is also easy to think that others are more affected than ourselves. In reality, all of us have been to some degree. By keeping this image of the splendor of heaven in mind, it should help us minimize that effect.

The Dimming of Our Eyes

An endless list dims the eye
of the splendor that will be.
When John was there, he fell as dead
when the Lord his eyes did see.

We'll see our God to whom we've prayed
and wondered all these years;
all will be in purest form,
there'll be no pain or tears.

The purest gold will form the streets
that the purest souls will walk;
we'll stroll beside the purest stream
while with other souls we'll talk.

We'll eat the fruit of the tree of life,
there'll be no tempter there;
the old is passed away for good,
the new is free of care.

Awesome thoughts to keep in mind
of heaven's pure comprise
would help us as we walk this earth
to fight the dimming of our eyes.

"Come out My people," He bids to us,
which suggests and does allude,
that even we, His chosen ones,
are targets to delude.

Easy to think so true of some
and miss our own demise,
but to some degree, we too are prey
to the dimming of our eyes.

6

Proverbs 14:12
There is a way that seems right to a man,
but in the end it leads to death.

Matthew 6:21
For where your treasure is,
there will your heart be also.

It is July 4. We are staying with friends on Kentucky Lake. We arrived a little late, and by the time we got here, everyone had either gone to town or had gotten out on the lake. Poor them! It just came a torrential downpour. I am sitting in a rocker on a covered porch, overlooking the lake. I see jet skis dashing around, a few boats, and one very nice cruiser anchored dead ahead.

The house in which we are staying, the jet skis, and the cruiser can either be God's blessing or a distraction from Him. Each individual must decide for himself whether, in his devotion to God, God has blessed him, or if in his devotion to things, God has let him have them. The owner of that cruiser may hunger and thirst for God; then again, he may not.

Our occupations have the same potential. A preacher may hunger and thirst for God; then again, he may not. He may be so busy doing things for Him that he fails to spend time with Him. A nurse, factory worker, doctor, or teacher may hunger and thirst for God; then again, they may not.

In whatever we have chosen to do in life, all have the same opportunity of what we will do with God. We can either hunger and thirst for Him, or we can keep Him at arm's length while we enjoy our things. If we choose the latter, we have settled for crumbs. We have allowed things to become a distraction.

If on the other hand, no matter who we are, if we keep Him first, He gives us these things to enjoy. Crumbs will never satisfy. There is always a need for more. The spot we are trying to fill with them was designed for God. First, fill that spot with Him, then keep that spot full of Him. Things in their right place will be more enjoyable.

We Settle for Crumbs

Unaware of the treasure
within our reach,
we settle for things
and for crumbs we seek.

No matter how good
we think our pursuits,
they pale in compare
to walking with You.

You've given us things
indeed to enjoy
but never were meant
our entire employ.

The diversions of life
have become our goal;
the space that was Yours
we no longer hold.

Unaware of the treasure
within each of our reach,
we settle for things,
and for crumbs we seek.

7

John 14:1
Do not let your hearts be troubled.
Trust in God.

Philippians 4:6, 7
Do not be anxious about anything, but in everything,
by prayer and petition, with thanksgiving,
present your requests to God.
And the peace of God, which transcends all understanding,
will guard your hearts and minds in Christ Jesus.

1 Peter 5:6, 7
Humble yourselves, therefore, under God's mighty hand,
that he might lift you up in due time.
Cast all your anxiety on him
because he cares for you.

Tied with the distraction of pleasure is the distraction of worry. So what's the harm of a little worry? Everyone worries. It's unrealistic to think we shouldn't worry at all. These and other thoughts like them are good examples of what Satan uses to counter what the Bible tells us about worry. "Do not be anxious about anything." Was that a misprint? Is the Bible unrealistic? Does it set too high a standard? If Satan can get you to think so, he has distracted you.

Worry is a result of believing that God can't. I wonder who suggests that. The Bible tells us we should go to God with any concern we have. I say we stay there until He gives us His peace. That is the harm of a little worry. We miss the peace He can and desires to give. We rob Him of the wondrous things He can do. We miss His best. When we listen to worry that says He can't, we are not giving Him the opportunity to show us that He can.

Be Anxious for Nothing

What worry today
has found a way in
and displaced trust
in the Master's plan?

It begins with a thought,
"I don't see how,"
"What will I do,"
or "There's no way out."

If Satan can get us
to focus on these,
then rather than him,
it's our trust that flees.

If we can focus
on God's Holy word,
Satan's deceit
will hardly be heard.

"Be anxious for nothing."
Can we comply?
Depends on our focus,
the truth or the lie.

I won't say it's easy.
It does take some nerve,
but it comes as we focus
on the One we're to serve.

8

Hebrews 12:7
Endure hardship as discipline.

Hebrews 12:10, 11
Our fathers disciplined us for a little while as they thought best;
but God disciplines for our good, that we may share in his holiness.
No discipline seems pleasant at the time, but painful.
Later on, however, it produces a harvest of righteousness
and peace by those who have been trained by it.

I have experienced God's punishment more often than I care to remember or admit. When there is a calling on your life to live right before Him, He is not after ballpark. He wants us holy. I'm convinced that some are called to a higher standard than others.

I think it is important to distinguish His discipline that is for the purpose of punishment and discipline that is for the purpose of refining. If the hardship or discipline points to some wrongdoing, it is punishment. Been there, done that, got marks to prove it.

But suppose you are seeking God and making good choices when a hardship comes along, the intent of that is not punishment; it's refinement. He sees good that could be better. Satan will try to convince you that it is punishment. There is always going to be something he can dig up. He does not play fair.

We may think we are okay. Compared to earlier years, maybe we are. But when God decides to take us to a new level, His fire reveals an awful lot of stuff that needs to change. He'll leave you dangling over it for a while, and it will seem like He doesn't care. It seems rather cruel at the time, but His sights are set.

It tests what you will do. Will you quit? Will you cling to Him in spite of the fact it seems He has turned His back on you? You feel you can't go on, but somehow you do. You feel He must show up, but He doesn't. Still you do not let go.

"No discipline is pleasant but painful." Oh, but afterward, and it is what He saw all along, "it produces a harvest of righteousness" and incredible peace. As bad as it got, you realize you made it through. Peter says, "He that has suffered in his body is done with sin." That is the effect. Sin has been burned away, and now the same trial begins to burn Him in.

God's Consuming Fire

We think we are clean till fire is applied.
It magnifies all that hasn't died.
It burns away sin throughout our test;
it's His require before His best.

We're used to His patience, His love, and His grace,
but in the fire, He hides His face.
Instead of mercy, seems mean and cruel;
we've now come under a different rule.

His sights are set on what is best,
good no longer His aim;
He stokes and pokes and throws on the coal,
and increases both heat and flame.

Once the fire has burned away
all that had not died,
a flood of grace is ushered in
as He shows up at our side.

The fire still continues to burn
but not to cleanse our sin;
where once it was there to burn away,
now it burns Him in.

PART 2

Strength for Our Trust

Just as there are specific things Satan uses to distract our trust, God has specific things that will strengthen it. In a nutshell, whether our trust is distracted or strengthened depends on whether we listen to Satan's lies or God's truth.

My morning routine consists of reading the Bible and then journaling my thoughts. Early in my test, I knew that I would need to spend more than my normal time with God to maintain my trust. Initially, trusting was a struggle. My two or three mornings with God each week soon turned into seven. In addition, I began to read more inspirational books and listen to more inspirational sermons.

One day, it dawned on me that I was struggling less. The verse "Faith comes by hearing" came to mind. I had been hearing so much more than normal that my faith and trust were stronger. Satan was having a harder time distracting me. I was experiencing the truth of that verse. The more we hear His Word, the more opportunity He has to speak to us. Conversely, the less we hear, the more opportunity Satan has to speak.

The Bible tells us, "Resist the devil and he will flee from you." Most of us are at least familiar with that verse and may feel it is all on us to go toe-to-toe with him to do so. One day, I was doing that very thing. He was working me over pretty good. I kept thinking of this verse and others as I tried to battle through his accusations and claims. But as all this was going on, God brought the other half of that verse to mind. "Draw near to God and He will draw near to you." He was calling me to Himself. As I focused my energy on seeking Him, Satan vanished.

I learned a very valuable lesson that day, which was made possible by being very familiar with God's word. We have been taught to resist Satan, and we should. He is the source of many thoughts that we need to recognize and resist. But occasionally he will bear down on us, and when that occurs, the more effective way to resist him is to draw near to God.

One night, I was talking about this with a friend of mine. To illustrate the point, I put God in the center of a field that was surrounded by a fence. Satan prowls the perimeter of the fence, trying to get our attention. As long as we stay at the center, focused on God, the things at the fence will not distract us. If those things (whether worry, pleasure, or any other thing) catch our eye, then the bottom line is our focus is drawn away from God. I liked my friend's comment. He said it was like staying in the eye of a hurricane. It's calm there. But venture out, away from center, and all hell breaks loose.

    I am convinced that the greatest strength for our trust is staying at the center with God. As we saturate ourselves in Him and in His word, we give Him an opportunity to speak His truth as Satan tries to deceive and distract us with his lies.

9

Genesis 46:3, 4
"I am God, the God of you father," He said. "Do not be afraid
to go down to Egypt, for I will make you into a great nation there.
I will go down to Egypt with you,
and I will surely bring you back again."

Exodus 14:13, 14
Moses answered the people, "Do not be afraid. Stand firm
and you will see the deliverance the Lord will bring you today.
The Egyptians you see today you will never see again.
The Lord will fight for you; you need only to be still."

Exodus 14:30, 31
That day the Lord saved Israel from the hands of the Egyptians,
and Israel saw the Egyptians lying dead on the shore.
And when the Israelites saw the great power
the Lord displayed against the Egyptians,
the people feared the Lord and put their trust in Him
and in Moses His servant.

God opened the door into Egypt for the young family that would eventually become the nation of Israel. It was a door that would stay open for a long time (four hundred years). It eventually closed, and when God closes a door, you will not open it again.

He's ready to take you to the next level. You will go there. You can do it kicking and screaming, or you can do it peacefully, but you are going. Sometimes He might open a new door before He closes one. How nice. Count yourself lucky when that happens. Other times, He might wait just a short time before He opens the next one. That's not too bad either.

But there is one more scenario; He closes one, and you guessed it, the next one does not open. What then? There is a reason, and no, it is not because He has a cruel streak in Him. He removes all your security because He wants you to learn to trust Him. Yes, it is scary at first, but the more you see His provision, the easier it becomes to trust. He will lead you through what seems to be impossible situations. Not to worry. That is His specialty.

It's one thing to try and hang on to trust in a situation that lasts for a short period of time, but when the days go on and on, every ounce of your ability to trust will be tried. You will be tempted to think there is no way. When that happens, let it be a red flag; that is exactly what it is supposed to look like. Remember that is His specialty. He wants to stretch your faith. Do not give up, no matter how hopeless it may seem. Look to Him. Look to His word. It may seem like He has abandoned you, but do not give up.

Between Two Doors

Are you waiting on God to open a door?
Has He closed the one He opened before?
Nothing is sure in this place in between;
what's going on, and what does it mean?

Uncertain our lot, we find ourselves forced,
to turn to the One that is our source.
He offers His light, but it doesn't reach far;
it seems just enough for right where we are.

Between the two doors, it must be His aim
to teach us to trust in Him to sustain.
Test after test, instead of relief;
This fast track to faith tries every belief.

We say we believe He's able to guide,
but can we still trust when He seems to hide?
We say we believe our needs He will meet,
but if daily He chooses, can we stay at His feet?

The next door is there, but the testing comes first;
in this time of our test will we hunger and thirst?
So do not lose hope; but continue to wait.
God will show up before it's too late.

10

Romans 10:17
So then, faith cometh by hearing, and hearing by the word of God.

1 Corinthians 10:6
Now these things occurred as examples
to keep us from setting our hearts on evil things as they did.

Exodus 14:21, 22
Then Moses stretched out his hand over the sea,
and all that night the Lord drove the sea back
with a strong east wind and turned it into dry land.
The waters were divided, and the Israelites
went through the sea on dry ground,
with a wall of water on their right and on their left.

When this period of between two doors began, I noticed my time with God intensified. I knew it was going to be tough and that I would need to stay closer to Him than normal, to stay strong through it. I knew Satan would try to make the most of it. When he did his best to discourage, I knew I would need to go to God for strength.

Satan is out to convince us of our doom. He has a pretty convincing argument. He's been at it a while. But God has things to say to us too. If we're not careful, we get so wrapped up in the lies that Satan is feeding us that we don't stop to give God a chance to give us His truth.

It is really that simple. God is very willing and able to help us and to do great things for us, but all too often, we cave in and take what Satan is saying, hook, line, and sinker. It must surely be a disappointment to God that we give up on Him before giving Him a chance. Think of it this way, you have given Satan your ear for a while; give God equal opportunity and see what He has to say.

The specific way I do this is by first reading His word. It will often speak to my situation, and I have the confidence of what He has said. It is what I focus on instead of what Satan has been saying. But also there are good books or inspirational sermons to read and listen to. All provide ammo to use against Satan when he suggests his lies. It helps us to recognize them more quickly.

This poem speaks of how incredibly creative God is and not just in creation. He still has all the creative ability He used in creation, waiting to be used to help us in what may seem to us, an impossible situation. Remember, that is His specialty. I have thought before, when Satan tries to tell me, "no way." In the back of my mind is, *Oh yeh, watch this.*

Faith Comes by Hearing

Faith comes by hearing. How much would you like?
The way has been set. It takes all your might.
Halfhearted is fine if in a tight spot you're not;
but in the midst of a test, it takes all that you've got.

Think on the stories of what He has done,
making a way when there seemed to be none.
The Bible is full of stories like these.
There are sermons and books, so listen and read.

Read of creation, of an earth without form;
He hovered and planned till order was born.
From a handful of dust, how complex we were made;
the sun for our warmth and trees for our shade.

Read about Israel against the Red Sea;
the perfect spot His wonders to see.
Though terror had struck, says, "All through the night,"
He protected from harm while preparing their flight.

All through our night of whatever we face,
He protects and provides while making our way.
These stories are written to help us believe,
for those who are able, their own to conceive.

God has not changed; He's still able to do,
but His hands are tied; He's waiting for you.
Build up your faith by hearing His word,
then do not back down; believe what you've heard.

11

1 Peter 5:8-10
Be self-controlled and alert. Your enemy the devil prowls around
like a roaring lion looking for someone to devour.
Resist him, standing firm in the faith . . .
And the God of all grace, who called you to His eternal glory in Christ,
after you have suffered a little while, will Himself restore you
and make you strong, firm and steadfast.

James 4:7, 8
Submit yourselves, then to God.
Resist the devil, and he will flee from you.
Come near to God and he will come near to you.

In the previous poem "Faith Comes by Hearing," the point is made of our faith being strengthened by a better diet of what we put into our mind. Reading the Bible and inspirational books are two excellent ways of boosting our general faith.

In this poem "The Battle for Our Faith," we have heard God speak. Faith has been conceived. Can we see it through to its birth or fulfillment? Satan will do all he can to counter it. The voice we listen to, whether Satan's deceit or God's truth, will determine who we believe and, therefore, who has won our faith.

It is not that clean and neat. In fact, it will likely get down and dirty. For example, I had been doing good to believe in spite of my test that God's hand was with me. Satan had tried repeatedly to convince me that God was in the process of wiping me out. I had pressed through all that and saw it as his attempt to get me to give up.

For some reason, I decided one day to read Ezekiel—bad decision. Just about the time I settle the issue that God is not going to wipe me out, I read a book of the Bible, which speaks of a time God is getting ready to wipe His people out. To make things worse, they were claiming His promises, which I was doing. God told them the promises they were claiming were of their own imagination. That created a toehold for Satan to use against me.

Had all my hope been my own imagination? It was an attack on the core of my belief. My faith was based on the thought that I had heard God promise He would protect and sustain. Destroy that hope, and there is nothing left to hang on to.

My challenge was to determine who was telling me it was my own imagination. It could have been God. After all, He had said it to this group of people. But it could also be Satan. He is the master of taking something like that and twisting it to help make his point. He twisted that one pretty good.

But I went to God and asked Him for the truth. This is what He showed me. The people this was about were living like hell. Yes, He was getting ready to wipe them out. Though they were living like hell, they were still claiming His promises. This part was huge. When that is the case, His words will not be about His promises; they will be about repentance. God's promises are for those who are living right before Him. If you are not, His words will be calling you to repentance. I had not been living like hell. So the promise I was claiming was from God. It was not a result of my imagination. This is a perfect example of how Satan tries to deceive, and how God, if we give Him a chance, can strengthen our trust.

Anytime God speaks to us, count on Satan to counter it. He is good at what he does. We are no match for him. The good news is we know the One who is. When Satan tries to discourage and distract you from what God has said, simply go to God and give Him opportunity to speak His truth. Satan can so thoroughly convince you that what he is saying is right, that you will feel there is no need to go to God. But give God a chance and see what wonders He will do to lift you. It is literally amazing.

The Battle for Our Faith

Faith comes by hearing, but what words have you heard?
Have you heard Satan's lies or the truth in God's word?
Both voices will speak, our faith on the line;
which one will you choose to believe in this time?

My God sent a test, forewarned, it would come;
a test of my trust like no other one.
I sought Him for help, I asked for relief;
till one day He said, I'll give you my peace.

You're not to ask for Me to provide.
I want you to trust and in Me confide.
I will sustain when it seems there's no way.
Can you trust what I've told you day after day?

But Satan speaks too to get his words in;
this is your doom because of your sin.
He's given you chances over the years,
but this time it's over; you'll pay more than tears.

God tells us His truth. Satan counters with lies.
Each after our faith; each equally vies.
How do we focus on the truth that we hear,
with lies so compelling, filling our ear?

I'll tell you a secret I've learned in my test.
It helps me to focus and stay in His rest.
When I sense he's at work and speaking his lies,
I draw near to God and stay close to His side.

I know He has truth and is waiting to say,
He knows He's my refuge and has strength for my day.
Our faith is restored by the One that we see.
Let God be your focus and in Him your faith be.

12

Matthew 3:16, 17
As soon as Jesus was baptized, he went up out of the water.
At that moment heaven was opened, and he saw the Spirit of God
descending like a dove and lighting on him.
And a voice from heaven said, "This is my Son, whom I love;
with him I am well pleased."

Matthew 4:1
Then Jesus was led by the Spirit into the desert
to be tempted by the devil.

Matthew 4:3
The tempter came to him and said,
"If you are the Son of God, tell these stones to become bread."

"Faith Comes by Hearing" emphasizes the importance of hearing things that inspire our general faith. "The Battle for Our Faith" emphasizes the battle we go through to maintain faith in something specific we have heard God speak to us. "When God Speaks" is about one such battle Jesus Himself fought. Anytime God speaks truth to us, count on Satan to counter it. Somehow, he will try to distract us from what God said.

Jesus had just heard God say, "This is my Son, whom I love; with Him I am well pleased." Even Jesus had mountaintop experiences, He had His share of valleys too and went immediately into one right after this feel-good moment. Matthew indicates that it was after Jesus had fasted forty days before Satan showed up. He is not stupid. Jesus had just heard God say, "This is my son." He was at His best when He entered the desert. It makes sense that Satan would wait for a weaker moment.

I have always thought that all this happens just as it reads. Satan approaches Jesus with these statements, and Jesus responds to each of them. It is possible. However, knowing that He was tempted in all ways just as we are, I wondered one day of the possibility of it all going down more like my experience. With me, it is all mental. He presents a thought in such a way as to make me think it is my own. That is part of the temptation.

Consider the possibility that this was a thought that came to Jesus's mind put there by Satan but, nevertheless, just the form of a thought. Remember the last thing Jesus heard God say, "This is my Son." Now the thought, *If you are the Son of God* . . . (I hope I do not lose you here), but try to imagine Jesus has been forty days without food. He is finally hungry. It is possible He feels the test is over. This thought comes to mind. If it's anything like the process I go through when a thought comes to mind, He had to determine its source.

Could it have been His thought? When I go through a desert experience, God usually makes Himself scarce. It can play tricks on your mind. Does Jesus, even if it is just for a split second, wonder to Himself, *If you are the Son of God?* In this critical moment of testing, does He possibly wonder if He is the Son of God and, on the heels of that thought, think that would be a way to prove that He is?

Or maybe, and again for just a very small part of that split second, does Jesus wonder if that thought could have come from His Father? Affirming the test was over, it could have been God's way of providing for His hunger. Affirming once again that Jesus is His Son, He is leading Him to turn these stones into bread.

And then all in the blink of an eye, He notices there was an "if" in that thought. If it was His thought, it expressed doubt. If it had been God, He would have said, "Since you are my Son." There is only one source left. Satan! He finally showed up. He waited until Jesus was at His weakest, but even then, Jesus was stronger.

We need to test our thoughts to determine their source. As faint as God's thoughts sometimes are, compared to Satan's blaring thoughts, we still need to test them to know which ones to hang on to. When we choose wisely, we can expect ministering spirits to come and strengthen us.

When God Speaks

"This is My Son, in whom I'm well pleased."
Upon hearing these words, enters desert with ease.
His spirit is stirred. He's prepared for the test,
but Satan's aware and thinks it not best.

"I'll wait till He weakens. I'll catch Him off guard.
At just the right time, it won't be so hard."
Forty days pass he never does show.
Hungry and weak, Jesus turns to go.

"Now is the time. My patience has paid.
I'll tempt Him to doubt what His Father has said."
At first He was sure. Now, maybe doubt's in His head.
"If you are His Son, you can turn this to bread."

"Wait just a minute. There was an 'if' in that thought?
Something is up. I believe I know what.
Satan, that's you. You finally did show.
At My weakest point, you gave it a go."

"But even when weak, I'm stronger than you.
Now get behind Me, and take what is due."
Then Satan left Him; angels came to His side.
God's strength they do bring for those who abide.

Very important to test the source of our thoughts;
they can easily mislead if we don't as we ought.
If we cling to the truth, Satan will go;
then angels will come, their strength to bestow.

13

Matthew 9:36
When he saw the crowds, he had compassion on them,
because they were harassed and helpless,
like sheep without a shepherd.

Matthew 23:2, 4
The teachers of the law and the Pharisees sit in Moses' seat.
They tie up heavy loads and put them on men's shoulders,
but they themselves are not willing to lift a finger to move them.

Matthew 23:23
Woe to you, teachers of the law and Pharisees, you hypocrites!
You give a tenth of your spices—mint, dill and cumin.
But you have neglected the more important matters of the law—
justice, mercy and faithfulness.
You should have practiced the latter, without neglecting the former.

I heard Brennan Manning speak once on *The Tenderness of Christ*. He was very interesting to listen to, but I caught myself thinking he was taking the tenderness thing a little too far. I thought maybe he was just trying to emphasize a point. I remember afterward, deciding to read the book of Matthew with an open mind to see what it said.

Plain and simple, he was not exaggerating. Over and over it says He was moved with compassion. But in the same book, He really let others have it. I never understood until this reading why he had compassion on some and was so hard on others.

The Pharisees and teachers were supposed to have a shepherdlike heart. Instead, they made it difficult on the masses by stacking laws upon laws that people had to live up to if they were to be pleasing to God. They made it so difficult that no one could measure up. They should have had justice, mercy, and faithfulness as their guide. Instead, they harassed and heaped on heavy loads.

Jesus had seen this from heaven for no telling how long. I think it was one of the reasons He came. He wasted no time, giving them the same medicine they had been giving the masses. He was merciful and had compassion on the masses because they needed it. Can you imagine the feeling, after all the years of hearing accusations, when Jesus told them they were the light of the world? Talk about a welcome relief.

So how does this relate to the strengthening of our faith? When you understand how the Pharisees were then, it can be paralleled with how Satan is to us today. It is Satan and not God that is forever demanding perfection. If he cannot get us to do wrong, he will demand so much right that we can never measure up. The result is that we always feel, no matter what we do, that we are not pleasing God. Understanding how opposed to this Jesus was, it helps us realize, first of all, that it is Satan. Jesus didn't like it then. He doesn't like it now.

To know Jesus was compassionate to those who had been harassed, and not condemning, is comforting and assuring now, as it is another piece of the puzzle in learning to recognize God's voice and guard against Satan's deceit.

The Master's Rage

For years I wondered of the Master's rage,
the harsh response on Holy page.
Where was compassion that others were shown?
What was the difference? What brought it on?

He had His fill of all He had seen.
The scales were tipped; He would right them again.
He was harsh to the harsh and rightly so.
They would finally reap what they had sown.

They heaped and harassed so that none could attain,
like wolves in the fold that unsettle and maim.
They offered no mercy, just more and more rules.
They had missed their purpose and in so became fools.

It is in this setting that the Master comes
with compassion for many, yet outrage toward some.
There wasn't a struggle with how to react;
He had seen it for years and came to attack.

It would cost Him His life, but oh what it bought;
there was peace for His sheep and hope for the lost.
Help us oh, Lord, to be careful with rules.
Let mercy and kindness be our choice of tools.

14

Matthew 5:6
Blessed are those who hunger and thirst for righteousness,
for they shall be filled.

Hebrews 11:6
And without faith it is impossible to please God,
because anyone who comes to him must believe that he exists
and that he rewards those who diligently seek him.

    In the overall general lack of hungering and thirsting for God today, our praying is shallow and less intense. We have so much that we really do not need God. We may have a bump now and then that might cause us to pray a little more intensely, but overall, we do not seek God.

    Missing is the hungering and thirsting for Him. This type of praying just seeks to know Him and to hear what He might say to us. We might have blind spots or things on which He wants us to focus that will make us more like Him. There might be things He wants us to pray about or things He just wants to show us about Himself. The list could go on and on. It is part of the transforming process that takes place when we spend time with Him.

    Too often, we settle for our own little laundry list of things that leave little room for any of the above. We do not have that much time. Life is good, and we'll take a little time to make it a little better hopefully. This type of praying really is shallow compared to what it could and should be like.

    It doesn't mean that we have to spend an hour praying for missionaries and world hunger. It is just simply spending time with God, reading His word to see what He might say to you, and then confiding in Him your innermost thoughts.

    The laundry list does Satan no harm. He'll give you all that you want. But this other sets you up to see God. It sets you up to see the little wonders He will do in and through your life. But first, you must hunger. If you hunger, you will be filled.

Today's Praying

Consider the prayers
we pray today,
prayers for help
and a better way.

What help do we ask
and way do we seek?
Will the help make us strong;
will the way lead us deep?

Are we content with the shallow?
Does the deep have no pull?
Are our minds set on ease
and things to the full?

Prayers that are shallow
yield shallow rewards,
Yet enough to suggest
we're okay with our Lord.

Is it possible, I've wondered,
as we pray our nest lined;
is it other than God
these thoughts come to mind?

What threat are these prayers
to Satan's main plan?
Our focus on ease
plays right in his hand.

He's more concerned
with those who are deep.
When they talk with God,
it's he who gets weak.

Fresh on their mind
are the wonders of God,
the heroes of old
and the steps they've trod.

All are examples
to show us the way
to our own set of wonders
from when we pray.

15

Ephesians 4:11-14
It was he who gave some to be apostles, some to be prophets,
some to be evangelists, and some to be pastors and teachers,
to prepare God's people for works of service, so that the body of Christ
may be built up until we reach unity in the faith
and in the knowledge of the Son of God and become mature,
attaining to the whole measure of the fullness of Christ.
Then we will no longer be infants, tossed back and forth by the waves,
and blown here and there by every wind of teaching
and by the cunning and craftiness of men in their deceitful scheming.

Ephesians 4:16
From him, the whole body, joined and held together
by every supporting ligament,
grows and builds itself up in love, as each part does its work.

The talents we have, whether singing, writing, speaking, or whatever has been given with the intent of using that talent for the building and encouragement of God's people. Many get diverted before they ever discover that.

A good singer may end up singing secular music. Instead of singing songs that inspire us to think of God's majesty or that encourage us to hold on through the storms of life, often the lyrics make us think of things we shouldn't. A writer or speaker has the same option.

In addition to talents, there are tendencies that we all have. Some are naturally generous, merciful, or helpful. All of these tendencies as well are God-given gifts to be used for the building of His kingdom.

As we all seek to know Him better, while sitting at His feet, He is able to guide and show us things to do, write, or say. As we all are mindful of His plan to use us in this way, we can seek Him with the hope of His showing us something we might do. The variety is endless. The things He will give us to do are unique to our situation. But we have to spend time with Him to learn what those things might be.

When Each Does His Part

God gives gifts
to strengthen and build,
His plan for His church
to know His will.

He gives teachers and preachers
and singers and poets
for the spreading of truth
in their way to show it.

Men and women
will sit at His feet
to learn from Him
what they might speak.

He gives helpers and givers
and encouragers too;
there are those who pray
and care and do.

All works together
when He's in command
and all do their part
as He had planned.

Whatever your strength,
do all to know it.
It's a God-given gift
for His church to grow it.

16

Mark 4:35-40
That day when evening came, he said to his disciples,
"Let us go over to the other side."
Leaving the crowd behind, they took him along,
just as he was, in the boat.
A furious squall came up, and the waves broke over the boat,
so that it was nearly swamped.
Jesus was in the stern, sleeping on a cushion.
The disciples woke him and said to him,
"Teacher, don't you care if we drown?"
He got up, rebuked the wind and said to the waves,
"Quiet! Be still!"
Then the wind died down and it was completely calm.
He said to his disciples,
"Why are you so afraid? Do you still have no faith?"

John 11:1, 3, 6, 21
Now a man named Lazarus was sick.
So the sisters sent word to Jesus, "Lord, the one you love is sick."
Yet when he heard that Lazarus was sick,
he stayed where he was two more days.
"Lord," Martha said to Jesus, "if you had been here,
my brother would not have died."

In the first story, the disciples end up in a pretty severe storm. Though Jesus did respond when they came to Him, He let it get bad enough that they did finally have to come to Him. In this situation, Jesus calms their storm, but He gives the disciples a little grief for not having faith that things would be okay. When they came to Him, they could have said, "Lord, we need your help. It's getting pretty bad out there." This would have at least shown they had faith in Him to keep them. Instead, they come with, "Lord, don't you care that we're going to drown?" There is absolutely no faith either in themselves or in Jesus. Jesus was silent for a period of time because He knew they were not in any serious danger. It looked bad, but He knew all would be well. He wanted them to have the same faith.

In the other story, Mary and Martha do have faith. They believe Jesus can heal Lazarus and send word for Him to come and do so. But Jesus stays where He is for two more days. Then there is travel time. By the time Jesus gets there, Lazarus has died and been buried four days. With the disciples, He calmed the storm. With Mary and Martha, He didn't. Jesus didn't come when they thought He should. Their hope became numb. Their faith had not paid. In fact, the situation got worse.

But in the end, in both cases, Jesus does eventually show up. In each case, those involved are drawn closer to Him and have a greater appreciation for Him. What He hopes is that until He does, we learn to trust Him and from that trust, be calmed.

When Jesus Doesn't Come

What's going on when Jesus doesn't come
in your time of need and your hope becomes numb?
All of the prayers and trust has not paid;
nothing has changed in this mess that's been made.

In fact when you pray, it seems to get worse.
"Cast all your care"; what's wrong with that verse?
It says "two or more" so you ask all your friends;
Surely, that's it, but it's nothing again.

You examine yourself and correct all you can,
in hope that you find what's holding His plan.
All options run out, you've tried every one;
what's going on when Jesus doesn't come?

When none of your pleas have evoked Him to do,
He's bidding you come; He has better for you.
He maintains His silence. He withholds His help.
He's trying to draw you in to Himself.

He rides in the eye of the storm as it blows;
the silence, His way of showing He knows.
He knows of the cup you've been given to drink,
and all of the doubt from all that you think.

With Me you'll find peace and the strength that you need;
I will get you through, if My words you'll heed.
The storm will not last forever you know,
and I offer you calm as through it you go.

17

Exodus 14:10
As Pharaoh approached, the Israelites looked up,
and there were the Egyptians, marching after them.
They were terrified and cried out to the Lord.

Exodus 14:19, 20
Then the angel of God, who had been traveling in front of Israel's army,
withdrew and went behind them. The pillar of cloud
also moved from in front and stood behind them,
coming between the armies of Egypt and Israel.
Throughout the night the cloud brought darkness to the one side
and light to the other side; so neither went near the other all night long.

    It is easy to claim, when things are going well, that God is able to provide and protect in our time of need. Even on the front end of a difficult situation, before the extent of the difficulty has reared its ugly head, we can proclaim the same with relative confidence. But let that difficulty either be extremely severe, even if short-lived, like the situation the Israelites found themselves in here, or a difficulty that spreads out over time that seems to have no end in sight, and everything we ever thought in relation to trust will be tried.

    In a twenty-four-hour period, Israel was carefree and on their way to a new place that God was taking them. They found themselves cornered with the Egyptian army breathing down their neck. There may have been a few that might have been thinking, *Okay, I wonder what God has up His sleeve here*. But I would say most were, as the verse says, "terrified."

    This situation came to a head quickly. In a matter of hours, they were in a do-or-die situation. Their faith was thoroughly tested. But what about a situation that just goes on and on. It might start out on the mild side. We might think early on, "I can handle this. I won't even flinch." But let that difficultly drag on. Let days turn to weeks, then months and maybe even years. Let what began rather mildly continue to get worse. Can you still not flinch?

    Both situations will try every fiber of our faith. When God is out to stretch your faith, He knows how to do it. It may be swift, or it may be drawn out, but

He knows how to do it. The swift ones, though they get to the point quickly, can leave us feeling like we have dodged a bullet when it is over. But let a test of time run its course, and you will think twice about feeling that way. The burning test of time will burn that one out along the way.

At first, in either case, we may feel like we are being dangled over a fire. But the place God wants us to get is the place where, even in the face of adversity, we can rest in the fact that He has us in the palm of His hand. He will lead us into or allow us to experience impossible situations so that He can show us they're not that impossible. There are examples such as these, plus ones of our own to help us learn how able He is to help, how able He is to protect, how able He is to provide.

It is one thing to write about it. It is one thing to say we trust when we are not being tested. But can you trust when you are? There is a place where you know that you know there is nothing too great for Him.

From the heart of Hudson Taylor, "So, if God should place me in great perplexity, must he not give much guidance; in positions of great difficulty, much grace; in circumstances of great pressure and trial, much strength? No fear that his resources will be unequal to the emergency! And his resources are mine—for he is mine, and is with me and dwells in me."

In Hudson Taylor's mission work in China, "faith was thrown into the crucible in many ways." Though they faced many difficulties, they refused "to look at difficulties rather than at the living God." It is truly possible to rest and trust while we wait on God's provision. In fact, that is what He wants us to do. The key to that place of rest is drawing close to Him and staying close to Him, giving Him opportunity to strengthen, encourage, and guide until He makes a way.

Why Do You Wait

Why do You wait
till our end is in sight
to show us the way
You've made in our night?

Backed to the sea
no apparent way out;
You settled for good
what Your might was about.

The trust that it takes,
when our end presses in,
tests every fiber
of belief that has been.

Easy to claim,
when all is okay
that You will protect,
that You'll make a way.

But can we still trust
when all is not well—
it doesn't take long
in a hardship to tell.

It can seem rather cruel
to dangle us so,
but if never a test
how else would we know?

Tests, You allow
and in them You wait.
Can we trust You to help
before it's too late?

Will we let go our claim
we made in our rest,
or can we hang on
all through our test?

He's after our trust—
for us to believe.
He offers us peace
until we receive.

18

Proverbs 3:5, 6
Trust in the Lord with all your heart
and lean not on your own understanding;
in all your ways acknowledge him,
and he will make your paths straight.

John 12:50
I know that his command leads to eternal life.

1 Peter 5:6, 7
Humble yourselves, therefore, under God's mighty hand,
that He may lift you up in due time.
Cast all your anxiety on Him because He cares for you.

There are two struggles when it comes to trusting God with our lives. First, we struggle with whether or not He even has a plan and then with whether or not we'll like it. Somehow, we feel that He is going to have us do something that will ruin our lives. We have come up with a much better approach that assures our happiness. We come up with our own plan and ask that He bless it. I'll bet He wishes He had thought of that.

The fact is, the One who created life knows a little more than we do about life. Recently, I read the verse I used above, "I know that his command leads to eternal life." It is only when we are aligned with His will and plan for our lives that we will be able to experience eternal, abundant life.

When we come to Him with our plan, He must surely roll His eyes and think, *Well, here's another one that we'll see years down the road.* No matter how good our plan might be, if it is not His plan, our lives will not be fulfilled. There will be something missing that we are constantly trying to fill.

He'll let us go, knowing that has to die before we will be willing to listen. At some point in life, after we have tried all, there is still the longing for something that we may not even know. We come back to Him for His help.

Finally, at a point that we are willing to listen, He begins to show us His plan. He begins to allow us to experience His life as we align ourselves with Him. It is what we have always longed for but looked for in other things.

He does still care. He has patiently waited for this to happen. He is still able to salvage your life. He won't hand it to you on a platter. There are tests and trials you will go through to determine your level of commitment. But if you come to Him and desire He direct your life, He will do it. When you come to Him on His terms, instead of your own, your life will have the abundance that you desire.

Can You Trust

Can you trust the One who knew how to bring
life from the dust of earth;
who brought the world we now enjoy
from darkness through its birth;

Who held the sea that His own could pass
while the enemy did pursue;
Who let it go at just the time
the enemy to subdue;

Who brought the water from the rock
when His people did complain
and the daily food that He sent
in order to sustain?

Can you trust in Him to meet your need,
whatever it might be,
or do you doubt He even cares
enough for one like "me"?

The struggle sometimes is not "if He can";
we know He has power still.
It's more a question in our case
of whether or not He will.

The key is spending time with Him
that your mind He can renew;
it is there you'll learn to hear His voice
and what He has for you.

19

Isaiah 43:25, 26

I, even I, am he who blots out your transgressions, for my own sake,
and remembers your sins no more.
Review the past for me, let us argue the matter together;
state the case of your innocence.

    It was our first vacation in a while. Vacations can be a time that we put God on hold, but not this time. He was as much a part of our going as we were. It was Florida, days before the summer season began. It was relatively quiet. We enjoyed walks, reading (and writing) around the pool, dinner out each night, and overall just a time of refreshing. We spent less money yet had a more enjoyable time than any vacation prior.
    A thought kept rolling around in my mind as I thought about the different frame of mind we were in. It wasn't drastic, but just enough to be noticeable. I could not imagine living in a way that He could be any more pleased with us, which is more than I could say about other times. We have had our share of times of being sidetracked and the scars to show for it.
    Hebrews 12 speaks of the discipline He uses to work in us His righteousness. I had had my share of it and felt it had finally taken. So the thought, if it is His intent to get us to live right, then when we do, shouldn't we experience His blessing. I liked that thought. Though I did not feel the current hardship was a punishment, still I enjoyed expressing this logical thought to Him in this poetic prayer.
    The Old Testament verse I have used came to mind the more I thought about this. He literally wanted them to bring their case before Him and argue their innocence. It was like He wanted me to do the same. I felt I had a very legitimate case. It was like we both enjoyed the discussion. Naturally, the hope was that this prayer and discussion would end our hardship.
    A few months have passed since then. Though He did not end the hardship, He made a way through it and gave us incredible peace in it. No matter how bad the situation seems to get, He matches it with His presence.

I have long since quit asking Him to make it go away. I know He could if He wanted to. But it is obvious He does not want to. Rather, He is content to protect and provide in it. If that is His chosen path, who are we to argue? We have seen His wonders; they're just not the wonders we thought we wanted to see, yet confident we will.

A Poetic Prayer

If you are intent
on punishing our sin,
then wouldn't right living
bring blessing again?

If it's Your goal
for us to live right,
then when we do,
would You not delight?

It's not our motive,
for that would be wrong,
but when right has been wrought,
for Your blessing we long.

It seems only fair,
all the whippings we've had,
to see some of the good
instead of the bad.

It wouldn't be right
to take every blow,
then Your care and Your love
for us not to know.

So I appeal to You now
in this poetic prayer,
in our time of need,
I ask You be there.

Show us Your strength
in a positive way.
Use it for good
the rest of our days.

Let us see wonders
of which we read.
Give us our own
for us to believe.

20

Hebrews 12:1-3
Therefore, since we are surrounded by such a great cloud of witnesses,
let us throw off everything that hinders
and the sin that so easily entangles,
and let us run with perseverance the race marked out for us.
Let us fix our eyes on Jesus, the author and perfecter of our faith,
who for the joy set before him endured the cross,
scorning the shame, and sat down
at the right hand of the throne of God.
Consider him who endured such opposition from sinful man,
so that you will not grow weary and lose heart.

I have read Hebrews 11 several times in addition to the specific events of which it refers. I have caught myself, being inspired by them, dreaming of similar opportunities to the ones to which He referred. Would God possibly speak to me as clearly as He did to Abraham when He told him to go to a land that He would show him? I would seek for that specific guidance. Time and time again, nothing came. Over time, I figured there was nothing that specific for me.

A few years ago, something began to stir in me. Though I did not stop attending church, I backed out of all my church duties. I was waiting on God to show me something about which I could once again get excited. Though I was not doing work for His kingdom anymore, I was seeking Him as never before. It has been the richest journey I have ever experienced. Many times I prayed that He would provide a ministry opportunity that was specifically tailored to me. There was a hungering and thirsting, though I did not know what He might eventually have for me. I knew that I knew that one day there would be something.

Of all the times I have read Hebrews, and as inspired as I have become at times by the stories of faith it speaks of, never until recently did I pick up on the little part of Hebrews 12:1 that says, "The race marked out for us." Each of the people referred to had run the race that had been set for them. That is the inspiration—not to want to do what they did, but to find the race that has been set for us.

I think the key is what was said of Moses. "He persevered because he saw Him who was invisible." We do not just seek Him for what He might have for us to do; we simply seek Him. As we get to know Him, we get to be familiar with His voice and His heart. Out of that will come the race He has set for us.

Let this "cloud of witnesses" inspire us to know the God they knew, the way they knew Him. That is where the birth of all faith begins. That is where our faith in what we have heard is strengthened and becomes unshakable because we have seen Him who is invisible.

The Cloud of Witnesses

Consider the cloud of witnesses
who spur us on to faith,
who've witnessed God enough to trust
and enter in His race.

Consider the land that Abraham left
for land he did not know,
but he knew his God and trusted Him
when He told him he should go.

Consider Hudson Taylor
and the race that was set for him;
he sought his God and heard Him speak
"Nothing this faith can dim."

The challenge though before us all
is our own race to find;
can we talk with Him enough to know
the thoughts He has in mind?

God has a plan for all who'll stop
and set their own aside,
but to find it we must walk with Him
before He will confide.

PART 3

Benefits of Our Trust

It only makes sense that if Satan is so intent on distracting us from our trust, and God is so intent on our trusting, the stakes must be pretty high. There are great benefits to finding it and, therefore, great misfortune if we do not. I have read of them many times, but until recently, I had never experienced them.

In John's gospel, the phrase "eternal life" is used several times. Often we think of that as being something to which we have to look forward when this life is over. That would be "everlasting life." But "eternal life" is something we can have now. John tells us that if we drink of the water He gives, which is the reading of His word, it will become a spring of water welling up into "eternal life."

It is available to anyone who is thirsty enough to come and drink. Many don't even come. Some sip. But you can come and drink as much and as often as you want.

One of the greatest benefits I have found in this trust is a rest from my efforts. I have worked hard all my life. I had to. We liked things. I have worked hard to be good enough to please God. Satan was constantly accusing me of my shortcomings. It all has literally worn me out. What a contrast to the picture painted by John, of Jesus our shepherd. His sheep have not a worry. He cares for them, protects them, and provides for them. He knows what they need and goes ahead of them to find good pasture they will enjoy. They simply trust. They go in and out without a care. I have found this shepherd, and rest in the trust that He cares. I have experienced His provision.

John tells us, "Do not let your hearts be troubled. Trust God." Jesus tells us, "I am the vine," and "apart from me you can do nothing." As hard as we try, we can do nothing. Nothing we can do on our own, can lead to this "eternal life."

Finally, John clarifies the meaning of "eternal life." "Now this is eternal life: that they may know You, the only true God, and Jesus Christ whom You have sent." To know God, to walk with Him, to talk with Him—all that we have hoped to find in our pursuit of things, yet don't, we find in Him. In Him is life to the full. That is what is on the line. "If any man is thirsty, let him come and drink."

21

Genesis 1:1, 2
In the beginning God created the heavens and the earth.
Now the earth was formless and empty,
darkness was over the surface of the deep,
and the spirit of God was hovering over the waters.

John 14:21 and 23
"He who loves me will be loved by my Father,
and I too will love him and show myself to him."
"If anyone loves me, he will obey my teaching.
My Father will love him, and we will come to him
and make our home with him."

One amazing thing about God's word is the living aspect of it. Why do certain things stand out sometimes and not others? Our attention may be drawn to a certain word or phrase. A thought may come to mind that we've never had before. When these kinds of things happen, I've learned to pay attention to them. Usually, it is God's way of letting me know there is something there He wants to show me.

It might be needed direction or encouragement. Something about a story will relate to your situation. It is one of God's ways of speaking. As much as Satan likes to speak and tear us down, God likes to speak and build us up.

An example of what I am talking about occurred not too long ago when reading the account of creation. For some reason, the idea of "hovering" stood out to me. I could not quit thinking about it. I thought about it for days. Days give you plenty of time to think a lot of thoughts. It is like the difference between soup out of the can and homemade soup that cooks all day. There is no comparison.

I thought in terms of possibly millions of years He might have hovered, which might explain some of the carbon dating that puts the age of some things at millions of years old. But more than that, I thought of what He might have been doing all that time. Possibly, He was planning creation. He planned the sun, moon, and stars and all the details associated with them. He did the same with plants, animals, fish, and birds. All the details that give us what we see today, He planned as He hovered.

When the time came, all that was left to do was speak into being all He planned. When He said, "Let there be light," it covered volumes of thought and planning. Though this thought did not give me guidance or encouragement for my situation, it was as if God was letting me in on a little something about Himself. It was just cool to think of it all. It was as if I had been allowed to walk and talk with the same God who had done all that I had just read about.

I didn't realize it at the time, but it ended up being a setup for something that was encouraging to my situation. As I was waiting on Him for something I needed to happen, He brought that word "hovering" to mind again. He used it this time to let me know that just as He hovered over the earth to plan its birth, so He hovers over us for the plan of our lives. While we wait, He hovers. All that is needed is for Him to speak His plan into action. How cool it is to walk with Him and trust in His plan.

God's Greatest Joy

For millions of years,
o'er a dark formless earth,
God hovered and planned
and devised its birth.

Pretty good plan,
wouldn't you say,
considering all
that is known today.

All of creation
was for His pleasure,
but one above all
exceeds all measure.

From the beginning of time,
the thing enjoyed most,
were the walks between man
and the heavenly host.

Nothing has changed
over the years.
We're a source of joy
or a source of tears.

Of all His creation
and majestic design,
our heart is still
the object in mind.

He still longs to walk
and talk as He did,
but far too many
keep themselves hid.

Still there are some
fortunate to find
the pleasure that was
in the beginning of time.

22

1 Thessalonians 5:17

Pray without ceasing.

    I have enjoyed the challenge of communicating in rhyme for years. Though my poetic inspiration has been a little sparse over the years, I have always enjoyed writing poems. I'm sure there have been years between poems, but when I woke up this particular morning with this thought on my mind, I had no idea that it would be the beginning of many more to come.

    "Pray without Ceasing" happened just as it reads. God was in my dream. When I woke up, my thoughts went seamless into a prayer. I could not help but to think, since not even night could end my praying, I was truly praying without ceasing. Before I got out of bed, I had the poem worked out in my mind. I got up, wrote down the words, and I do not believe they have changed.

    Within the next day or two, I was writing "Seek Ye First." No sooner than I had finished it, I was writing "The Lure of Good Things." They just kept coming. There were times I was working on three at a time. It was quite different from sometimes being a year or more between poems.

    I wish I could say they all came as easy as "Pray without Ceasing." That one came literally in minutes. Others I have labored over for weeks. I have labored over them for days and, in the end, delete all but the title and then start over. I took three weeks to write the first half of one and then the second half came in about an hour.

    I began to wonder after I had written about twenty, if there was a purpose for them that was beyond just my own enjoyment. I had prayed a few years before, and many times since, that God would provide an opportunity that was specifically tailored to me that I could once again be excited about.

    Part of the seeking process involved journaling my thoughts. I had come to thoroughly enjoy writing. I wondered if somehow He had a plan for the things I had written that would somehow be the opportunity I had prayed for.

    I believed the experiences I was having were for a purpose beyond myself, but as of yet, I did not know what that purpose was. I knew that He was leading, but to where I did not know.

Pray without Ceasing

I awoke from my dream
in which You were there.
Seamless my thoughts
turn into prayer.

All through the day
and night does not end,
this communion I've found
as friend talks with friend.

23

Ephesians 2:1-5
As for you, you were dead in your transgressions and sins,
in which you used to live when you followed the ways of this world
and of the ruler of the kingdom of the air,
the spirit who is now at work in those that are disobedient.
All of us also lived among them at one time,
gratifying the cravings of our sinful nature
and following its desires and thoughts.
Like the rest, we were by nature objects of wrath.
But because of His great love for us, God, who is rich in mercy,
made us alive with Christ even when we were dead in transgressions—
it is by grace you have been saved.

Ephesians 4:17-19
So I tell you this, and insist on it in the Lord, that you must no longer
live as the Gentiles do, in the futility of their thinking.
They are darkened in their understanding
and separated from the life of God
because of the ignorance that is in them
due to the hardening of their hearts.
Having lost all sensitivity, they have given themselves over to sensuality
so as to indulge in every kind of impurity, with a continual lust for more.

Ephesians 5:8
For you were once darkness, but now you are light in the Lord.
Live as children of light.

    I was talking with someone one day. My interests had changed since the last time we were together. I didn't mind so much that his hadn't; it's just that mine had. He had not been dangled over a fire like I had been.
    But one thing did strike me as we talked; there had to be more that was different about my life than some things I no longer did. There had to be life that was not there before. If the change that had taken place in me did nothing

more than cause me to not do some things that I used to do, what is the appeal of that? There had to be life. I remember praying as we talked, "Lord, let there be good in my life that would draw others to You."

The second half of this poem is the essence of what I prayed as a result of the experience. It is a prayer that our lives, once we truly encounter God, will be marked by new things we do more than by the old things we no longer do.

There is a place for us being different in the things we no longer do. It should be so. I believe the church has lost its distinction in that area. It is getting harder and harder to tell the church from the world. That needs to change.

But the way to that change is that we first encounter God. It is not just a determination to not do this or that, although there is a place for that. That alone does not last. It is as we encounter God that He changes us. He imparts His life to us. As that happens, the new life weeds out the old. As we experience the wonder of God and the wonders from God, that becomes the life and light we have to offer the world. If all we have is "don't do this and don't do that," we have fallen far short of His intent when He said, "Live as children of light."

A Different Path

We're called to walk a different path
than those who do not know;
should effect the things we do and say
and places that we go.

But if we go and do and say
the same as most of them,
we're not the light that we should be;
instead, we just blend in.

Help us Lord to be the light
and salt that we should be;
not to point at all the faults,
instead, the good to see.

Enrich our lives on this different path
more than what we don't do;
fill us with good that others may see
and be drawn by it to You.

24

Exodus 40:36, 37
In all the travels of the Israelites,
whenever the cloud lifted from above the tabernacle,
they would set out; but if the cloud did not lift, they did not set out—
until the day it lifted.

Philippians 4:6, 7
Do not be anxious about anything,
but in everything, by prayer and petition,
with thanksgiving, present your requests to God.
And the peace of God, which transcends all understanding,
will guard your hearts and your minds in Christ Jesus.

When Israel was experiencing their time between two doors, God led them with a cloud. When the cloud lifted and moved, they would move with it. If it did not move, they stayed put.

It is not always that easy with us. We may try to seek God's guidance, but often, if we do not get an answer right away, we assume He's not going to give one, and we make our own decision. But maybe He did give it. From the text above, it was very plain. If the cloud lifted and moved, they moved. If the cloud did not lift and move, they stayed put. If God has not given you His direction, it is His way of saying, "stay put."

Our problem is that we try it. You can't try it. You have to be committed to it. God is very able to make His way clear. We have to be committed to waiting until He does. There has to be an abandoning of self-reliance. We've all probably had times when He has made His way clear; it is cool when He does. It is especially cool when you have had to wait. It may go against all reason, but until He gives you His peace, stay put.

I had a job opportunity not too long ago. It was a very good one. For some reason, I did not feel at peace about it. It got to a point that when I would think about it, there was a distinct 'no' associated with it. It really didn't make sense. It was a big deal to turn it down. If I was wrong, I would look foolish for one. For another, I could be missing out on God's provision.

Knowing how big a decision it was, I asked for one more source of confirmation. There were a couple of other possibilities brewing. I felt He could make one of them rise to the surface, and that would be His direction. In this case, one of the possibilities did surface. It was His clear confirmation. To this day, I have never doubted the decision to let the opportunity pass.

He is able to guide and make His way clear. To experience it, we must abandon all to His discretion, judgment, and timing.

What to Do

Ever wonder
how to know
if it is time to stay
or it's time to go,

if what you're doing
is what you're to do,
if there's something else
that's right for you?

Are you trying to trust
in the Lord to guide,
but instead He seems
content to hide?

He hasn't abandoned
nor is He sleeping;
He hovers and plans
for our safekeeping.

He may not be early
but He will not be late.
Though His help lingers,
continue to wait.

Trust in Him fully.
He will let you know,
when it's time to stay
and when it's time to go.

Don't let impatience
force you to do;
It will cause you to miss
His best for you.

25

Acts 14:3
So Paul and Barnabas spent considerable time there,
speaking boldly for the Lord, who confirmed the message of his grace
by enabling them to do miraculous signs and wonders.

Acts 15:12
The whole assembly became silent
as they listened to Barnabas and Paul
telling about the miraculous signs and wonders God had done
among the Gentiles through them.

Acts 20:22, 23
"And now, compelled by the Spirit, I am going to Jerusalem,
not knowing what will happen to me there.
I only know that in every city the Holy Spirit warns me
that prison and hardships are facing me.

"The whole assembly became silent as they listened to Barnabas and Paul telling about the miraculous signs and wonders God had done among the Gentiles through them." Can you recall the last time you sat and listened to someone telling about the wonders that God had done in or through them? Isn't it just as cool as it can be?

God is still very much in the "wonder" business. However, I think the church has, for the most part, lost its sense of the wonder of God. Though these wonders still occur, I think they occur in far too small a group. For the majority, I think there is a range of rarely to not as often as they should.

In the absence of these wonders, I think we have gone after things and then attribute them as God's blessing. There is a desire to feel we are right with God. So if the wonders are not there, we can hang our hat on His blessings. In many cases, though, these so-called blessings aren't really blessings at all. We have gone after things with incredible energy and gotten them. The question we have to answer is this: are the things we have a result of our dedication to God, or in our dedication to things, has God allowed us to have them?

Many of us have things. Many claim they are the blessings of God. Is that really solid evidence of His blessing? Is there a way to know? I think there is. For starters, if you're seeking things more than God, they are not His blessings. "Seek ye first his kingdom." "The blessing of the Lord makes rich, and he adds no sorrow with it." If our things are not His blessing, they will be a distraction from Him. If they are not His blessing, there will likely be stress in trying to hang on to them while at the same time, we are going hard after more.

If you're seeking God first, and I do mean first—first as in the same level of intensity that things have been pursued—things will lose their appeal. But the cool thing is that He will begin to give you things. It may not be the deluge you are used to, but they will be sweet. It is truly a case of "less is more."

But the coolest part of all are the wonders we see Him do in and through us. We, as common believers, may not see people come back from the dead or see miraculous healings, but nevertheless, we will see wonders. Unmistakable acts of God in our lives will occur on a regular basis. Whether it is the way a need is met, the way He directs us, or the little opportunities He puts before us, it will be undoubtedly Him.

There is a reason that everything in us fights against a canned presentation of Christ. It was never intended to be canned. When Jesus told the disciples they were to be witnesses, it simply meant they were to tell about the things they had personally witnessed. When we have seen and experienced our own set of wonders, it is as natural talking about them to others as the latest game we watched or deal we found at the mall.

His wonders in our lives are the only substantial evidence of His blessing on our lives. Whether rich or poor, ditchdigger, or doctor—not all would be labeled a success, but all could experience His wonders.

In J. I. Packer's book *A Passion for Faithfulness: Wisdom From the Book of Nehemiah*, which is the only book I have read twice, he quotes from the poem "If" by Rudyard Kipling.

> *If you can meet with Triumph and Disaster*
> *And treat those two imposters the same.*

We often treat triumph and disaster, success and failure as God's blessing or curse on us. Neither is necessarily the case.

Success is not an end in itself. Failure is not the end. We don't hang our hat on success or our head on failure. God is to be our all no matter what. If He is, He will be in our success. If He is, He will be in our failure. Whether we are experiencing what the world considers success or what it considers failure, we should have His wonders in our life. That then becomes the only substantial evidence of our lives being pleasing to Him.

God's True Blessing

How is God's blessing
determined today?
Is it an increase at church,
in business, or pay?

Is it in a good job,
good husband, or wife;
two kids and a pet,
would that suffice?

How about a nice home
in a nice part of town
and a few good friends
that won't let you down?

An absence of hardship,
things going well,
the list could go on,
is this how we tell?

Of all the things listed above,
Jesus had one or two,
but of all the things His list contained,
most have just a few.

He had no home, no wife, or kids,
no wealth of which to speak;
but everywhere that He went,
God's wonders He did see.

And then there's Paul, who's walk with God,
began when stricken blind;
full attention now obtained,
God's calling he did find.

This calling did not bring Him wealth,
but there was a little fame;
instead God showed him he would suffer
for preaching in His name.

For preaching he was put in jail,
beaten and left for dead,
but signs and wonders confirmed the grace
God put upon his head.

The disciples who had followed Him
in hopes of earthly fame,
once that hope of fame was gone,
received power to proclaim.

That power seems to only come,
when other hope is lost;
it is then we seek with all our heart,
it's Him at any cost.

We may lose things, but count them not,
in light of what He gives.
God's true blessing is His wonders;
they confirm our calling lived.

26

John 16:33
"I have told you these things, so that in me you may have peace.
In this world you will have trouble.
But take heart! I have overcome the world."

Romans 8:35
Who shall separate us from the love of Christ?
Shall trouble or hardship or persecution or famine or nakedness or danger or sword?

Romans 8:37-39
No, in all these things we are more than conquerors
through Him who loved us.
For I am convinced that neither death nor life,
neither angels nor demons,
neither the present nor the future, nor any powers,
neither height nor depth,
nor anything else in all creation,
will be able to separate us from the love of God
that is in Christ Jesus our Lord.

Praise You In This Storm by Casting Crowns

I was sure by now
That you would have reached down
And wiped our tears away
Stepped in and saved the day
But once again, I say "Amen," and it's still raining

As the thunder rolls
I barely hear You whisper through the rain
"I'm with you"

And as your mercy falls
I raise my hands and praise the God who gives
And takes away

I'll praise you in this storm
And I will lift my hands
For You are who You are
No matter where I am
Every tear I've cried
You hold in Your hand
You never left my side
And though my heart is torn
I will praise You in this storm

The words to this song, written by Mark Hall, so accurately express the longing we have for God to come in and save the day. As Mark says in his introduction to the song, "Sometimes God calms the storm. Sometimes He chooses to ride them with us." The opening lines of this song was the inspiration for the opening lines of my poem.

It is natural for us to want Him to come in and save our day. Why wouldn't we? We want to see the grand that we know He is capable of doing. We want our own stories to tell of His wonders. Admirable desires but as often the case, whatever we imagine is usually so very different from what God has planned.

It would be easy to think, when He does not step in and save our day, that He is not mindful of us, that He does not care. But oh, the touch that we miss if we stop there. It is beyond our ability to imagine when He does not step in, that what He intends to do can be better.

Is His peace only available when things are good? Who but God can give it to us through our darkest moments? It is unimaginable, but then, that is what God is good at. He longs for us to look to Him in whatever we face. He longs for us to trust that He is able to sustain no matter our lot.

Nothing has to separate us. We let it happen. But if we listen closely, we can hear Him "whisper through the rain, I am with you." If He is with us, what can happen that He cannot handle? What can happen that He cannot give us the strength to endure?

Daily versus Grand

I would never have dreamed
when all this began
that we'd still be waiting,
that this was Your plan.

I had hoped to see wonders
of which we'd proclaim.
We'd have our own stories
of the power in Your name.

Instead of the grand
that so many would see,
He had daily provision
in store for me.

He would teach me to trust;
more important to Him,
He would show me a faith
the world could not dim.

So sweet this walk
as daily I lean,
I now know firsthand
what your peace can mean.

My hope has now changed
though the grand I would take,
give me the daily,
and the grand I'll forsake.

27

John 4:13, 14
Jesus answered, "Everyone who drinks this water will be thirsty again, but whoever drinks the water I give him will never thirst. Indeed, the water I give him will become in him a spring of water welling up into eternal life."

John 7:37, 38
"If anyone is thirsty, let him come to me and drink. Whosoever believes in me, as the Scripture has said, streams of living water will flow from within him."

John 8:47
He who belongs to God hears what He says.
The reason you do not hear is that you do not belong to God.

John 8:59
At this, they picked up stones to stone him, but Jesus hid himself, slipping away from the temple grounds.

Jesus is the well of life. He offers to anyone who would come and drink, life that is described as streams of living water. The Pharisees, who didn't recognize Him for who He was, threw stones at Him. Others, who did, believed Him and came to Him and drank from the well.

Still there is another group who came to the well but never really drank from it. They may have wanted to, but Satan would wrap them up a million ways to keep them from it.

Before I became a Christian, I threw stones with the rest of them. But I have to admit once I became a Christian and came to the well, somehow Satan kept me from its streams of living water. I enjoyed trickles now and then, but there was more wishing at the well than drinking from it.

Not until recently could I say that I have not only come to the well, but that I come often enough and stay long enough to actually be filled and satisfied from it. I have read and studied the Bible off and on since becoming a Christian.

I have taught Sunday school for my age-group. I knew there was life there. I enjoyed it at times. But Satan was always able to distract me just enough that I was not able to regularly enjoy the abundance that is available.

I think a battle does rage when we become a Christian. Satan knows what is at stake. If he can hinder, he will. He is the father of lies. If we listen to them, he may distract us for years. He did me.

The Well

I once threw stones at the well of life;
I was blind and could not see.
And then the well made sense one day;
I wondered, "Could it be?"

So I dropped the stones and drew in close,
tossed coins and wished to find,
this life it spoke and offered to all,
I wished to make it mine.

But a fight broke out and a battle raged
to keep me from this well;
it appeared my choice had raised the brow
of all the force of hell.

"Stand at the wall and toss your coins,
but that's as far as you will get.
We'll wrap you up a million ways,
no further will we let."

Years have passed, and I must confess
that what they said, they did;
they let me stand by the well of life,
but its life they somehow hid.

But now I know and clearly see
the life I now have found;
I was finally thirsty enough to come
and would not turn around.

It is for all who will come,
if you're thirsty, come and drink;
if you're not, there'll be other things,
in them is life you'll think.

You'll stand at the well and toss your coins
and wish for abundant life;
as years fly by you'll wish away
while caught up in the strife.

Come to the well and do not leave
until you have been filled;
careful the voice you listen to,
lest years go by until.

28

Hebrews 4:9-11
There remains, then, a Sabbath-rest for the people of God;
for anyone who enters God's rest also rests from his own work,
just as God did from his. Let us, therefore,
make every effort to enter that rest,
so that no one will fall by following their example of unbelief.

1 Peter 5:10
And the God of all grace, who called you to his eternal glory in Christ,
after you have suffered a little while,
will himself restore you and make you strong, firm and steadfast.

After years of my "own work," it is sweet to rest. I have worked to be good enough. I have worked to make things work out. I simply have worked. I'm convinced that we do not enter His rest because we do not know how. Because we aren't convinced that He will do for us, we take it upon ourselves to do for ourselves.

Satan is a big part of it. He is the father of lies. He feeds us lies continuously, at least, as long as we will believe them. But God in His mercy sees the merry-go-round we're on and brings it to a halt. It is spinning out of control, and it is getting harder and harder to hang on. We have suffered long enough. We are at a place where we are hungry to enter His rest.

The rest does exist, and God is pleased when we are ready to find it, to allow us to enter it. He cleans us and takes away our sin. It no longer has the pull that we must work to resist. He knows our needs and provides for them. It is no longer up to us to go after them. It is plain and simply a rest from our "own work."

Having lived on the other side of this rest for years, I appreciate the find. Having read of it in Hebrews recently, the thought of it was fresh on my mind. I wanted to write a poem about it, which is how I spend some of my leisure. But this particular day, the Lord bid me play in my leisure. My wife and I went into town a little early, had an early dinner, then browsing through a bookstore, I found a book.

The book was about Hudson Taylor who I was at least a little familiar with. So I was intrigued when I saw the title. I could not believe my eyes when I opened it and found the poem they had used as the opening for the first chapter. I wanted to write a poem about His rest. But God, to emphasize the point, bid me rest and instead showed me one He had written years before. It was a cool moment and, I must say, one of the richest books I have read to date—*Hudson Taylor's Spiritual Secret*.

"Thy Work—To Rest in Me"

My thoughts were turned toward His rest;
I thought a poem to write.
Would have labored long and hard I guess,
would have tried with all my might.

But I guess to emphasize the point
of resting more in Him,
He bid me play in my free time,
which led me to this gem.

I like to put my thoughts to rhyme;
it's just the way it is.
But it seemed to please Him in this case
to show me some of His.

Had I written my own I'm sure,
been twenty lines or more,
but He said it all and made the point
and it only took Him four.

Bear not a single care thyself,
One is too much for thee;
The work is mine, and mine alone;
thy work—to rest in me.

—Unknown

29

Isaiah 26:3
Thou wilt keep him in perfect peace, whose mind is stayed on thee: because he trusteth in thee.

John 10:9, 10
I am the gate; whoever enters through me will be saved.
He will come in and go out, and find pasture.
The thief comes only to steal and kill and destroy;
I have come that they may have life, and have it to the full.

Very much like the last introduction and poem, there is a place of trust in God that is beyond what most are able to find. Still, it exists. It does require a complete abandonment of self-reliance. Until we reach that place in our lives, which I refer to as "coming to the end of ourselves," we will not experience what this poem claims.

I play golf two or three times a year. I know what it is like to hit the "sweet spot" of the club. It has a different sound to it, a different feel to it, and, best of all, a different result from it. There is a tendency when we have hit that sweet spot, to add a little more of our power the next time, to make the ball go even a little farther. It might very well, but it also might be in the wrong direction. An easy swing and a solid hit in the "sweet spot" is the best combination. Knowing this as much as I do, I still want to add a little more "umph" at times, but usually not a good idea.

God reserves His best for those who abandon trust in themselves and trust wholeheartedly in Him. He gives them peace as they wait on Him because they trust Him. He is the Great Shepherd. He protects and provides for His sheep. He knows the pasture they need and goes ahead of them to find the best for them. His sheep know His voice. They follow Him as He leads. They go in and out to enjoy the pasture He provides. They have found the sweet spot and do not try to add to it. "He gives the very best to those who leave the choice to him."

"Enough That God My Father Knows"

Another gem He gave to me,
truth that comes from Him;
He longs for those who will trust
and their own thought see as whim.

Can you trust in Him to guide your life
or to your own thoughts do you cling;
there first must be a letting go
to see what He will bring.

The gem I speak that He let me find;
His guidance then for me,
the yearning of His heart in words
that express how things can be.

He truly longs for us to rest
and wait upon His lead,
a treasure beyond any dream
if this advice we heed.

Enough that God my father knows:-
Nothing this faith can dim.
He gives the very best to those
who leave the choice to Him.

—Unknown

30

John 4:13, 14
Jesus answered, "Everyone who drinks this water will be thirsty again, but whoever drinks the water I give him will never thirst. Indeed, the water I give him will become in him a spring of water welling up to eternal life."

John 10:14
I am the good shepherd; I know my sheep and my sheep know me.

John 12:50
I know that his command leads to eternal life.

John 17:3
Now this is eternal life: that they may know you, the only true God, and Jesus Christ, whom you have sent.

As you may have gathered by now, our testing has been the result of a stormy hallway experience. In it has been an adequate supply of both trouble and hardship. God closed one door in our life, and we wait in the hallway for Him to open another. At first, I sought Him for the door He might open. My trust was in Him. I believed that He would.

In the course of my seeking though, I found Him. There were times, He was all I wanted. He gave me water that became in me a spring of water, welling up to eternal life. After referring to "eternal life" several times in his gospel, John finally clarifies what it is, "Now this is eternal life: that they may know you, the only true God, and Jesus Christ, whom you have sent."

We have many acquaintances but few very close friends. When God becomes closer to us than an acquaintance, and we know Him as much or better than our closest friends, that is eternal life. By spending as much time with Him as I had, I had come to know Him in a way that I never had before.

I found the Shepherd who cares for His sheep. He looks after them and finds pasture for them. He knows what they need. This then becomes the door to all other doors. I no longer seek the Shepherd for the door He might open, I simply seek the Shepherd who opens all doors. My only duty is to remain close and listen for His voice. I know that His voice/command leads to eternal life. It is so very critical that we take time to listen for it. To hear His voice is truly our only need.

This My Only Need

I sought a door to open first
to replace the one that closed,
but my search has found two other things,
my searching now transposed.

Along the way I found a well;
in my thirst I stayed to drink.
So sweet the waters to the taste,
the door I did not think.

I found a shepherd who let me in
to the fold for which he cared,
and again the door for which I sought
I forgot while I was there.

This well and shepherd that I've found,
the source of life for me;
my seeking now has been transposed,
what door could better be?

No longer do I seek the door,
but the well and waters sweet;
I seek the shepherd who cares for me;
my every need to meet.

This the door to other doors
through which in time He'll lead,
but now my part to follow close,
this my only need.

31

John 10:7
Then said Jesus unto them again, "Verily, verily, I say unto you,
I am the door of the sheep."

John 10:3-5
The watchman opens the gate for him,
and the sheep listens to his voice.
He calls his own sheep by name and leads them out.
When he has brought out all his own, he goes ahead of them,
and his sheep follow him because they know his voice.
But they will never follow a stranger; in fact,
they will run away from him because they do not recognize a stranger's voice.

"For Those Who Hear His Voice"—we all hear it, and we all respond to it in different ways at different times in our lives. He sows, and sometimes, it is snatched up before we even think about it. Sometimes we get excited about what we've heard but fizzle quickly. Sometimes our heart is not right when we've heard, and we choose to not listen.

Oh, but when our heart is right and we do hear. How fortunate we are that God does not give up on us. He continues to speak in hopes that one day we will hear. He allows hardships to come into our life as opportunities to see if we are ready to listen. Some will not. They press through on their own. Some will listen and seek His way for their future.

He may open a door quickly. If He does, be thankful for it. That is His plan for you at the moment. Enjoy it and do not forget Him in it. He may not open a door quickly. If He does not, it may be that He is leading you to a place that few people find. It is a place of total dependence on Him and complete trust in Him.

It does not come easy, but somehow, He assures you that you are on the right path. There will be fierce battles with Satan because he knows what is in store. It requires a focus on God like you have never known. The focus is critical. The same focus that is required to withstand Satan's attacks is still required later to enjoy His rest. But once you have experienced it, it is worth all you have had to go through.

In this place, Satan's influence is almost nonexistent. You have become very aware of his ways and recognize them quickly. You no longer listen to his lies. Instead, you hear the voice of God, and in it is life. There is no better place to be.

As this book has been about a stormy place between one door that has been closed and the other that is not yet opened, I believe, though there has been no physical breakthrough, the door He has opened is one to Himself. He knows not only what I need, but also what He has planned for me. I have come to a place where I trust Him for both. It is a place of trust in the center of the storm, and at the center with God is peace.

For Those Who Hear His Voice

Between two doors is a defining place;
    it tests what you believe.
What you had is gone for good;
    your future just conceived.

Will you trust in God alone,
    your course to now direct,
or will you cling to familiar things
    and miss what He has next?

Unfortunate the one who does not look
    to Him for what He's planned;
he charts his course himself instead
    and on his own he stands.

Better the one who looks to God
    and hopes His open door;
he seeks Him hard in his time of need
    for what He has in store.

Still there is one who as he seeks
    for the door He has in mind,
discovers yet a better door;
    the Master he does find.

"I am the door," He tells His own;
    His own will hear His voice.
He goes ahead and prepares the way,
    and they follow and trust His choice.